Original title:
Snowlight Embrace

Author: Kätriin Kaldaru
ISBN HARDBACK: 978-9916-79-360-2
ISBN PAPERBACK: 978-9916-79-361-9
ISBN EBOOK: 978-9916-79-362-6

Embracing the Frosted Universe

Stars twinkle in the chill,
Whispers ride the night air,
Each breath a puff of frost,
Wrapped in winter's care.

Silent trees stand tall and bare,
Moonlight glints on silver ground,
Nature's canvas, pure and bright,
In silence, peace is found.

Gentle winds weave tales of old,
Stories shared with every flake,
Magic dances in the cold,
Awakening from slumber's wake.

The universe, a frosted dream,
Galaxies in icy embrace,
Every crystal shines and gleams,
In dark, we find our place.

Together we become the night,
Stitched in starlight, hand in hand,
Embracing this frost and light,
In this vast, cold wonderland.

Hush of the Snow-Blanketed Earth

A hush falls over the land,
Soft whispers of falling snow,
Each flake a gentle caress,
In moments, the world slows.

Blankets of white wrap the ground,
Quieting every sound,
In this serene silhouette,
Peace and comfort abound.

Footprints trace a simple path,
Leading to a world anew,
With every step, magic grows,
In the soft, white hue.

Branches bow beneath their load,
Crystals glisten in pale light,
Nature rests, calm and still,
Embracing the frosty night.

In this slumber, dreams take flight,
Warmed by the cool, soft air,
The earth, a canvas vast and wide,
Invites us to linger there.

Shards of Light in the Frost-Bound Evening

Crimson skies turn to deep blue,
As day melds into night,
Shards of light pierce the twilight,
In a dance of pure delight.

Frost grips the edges of time,
Each breath hangs like a song,
While shadows stretch and linger,
Where the chilly winds belong.

Stars emerge, one by one,
A tapestry woven above,
Guiding hearts through the darkness,
In their flicker, is our love.

The world is cloaked in quiet,
Each moment feels so right,
In the frost-bound evening's glow,
We find warmth in the night.

Together we share this view,
As the stars start to twinkle,
In shards of light, hearts ignite,
In the winter’s gentle sprinkle.

Celestial Hues of Icebound Wonder

Colors blend in the cool air,
Icy blues and silvers glow,
Heaven's palette brushed wide,
In the moonlight's soft flow.

Everything sparkles under stars,
Violet shades aux courage,
Each icy drop a glimmer,
With a touch of homage.

Here beneath celestial skies,
Whispers of magic unfold,
Nature's secrets wrapped in light,
In the elegance of cold.

The night is alive with wonder,
Every sparkle tells a tale,
Of dreams woven in the frost,
By the moon's gentle sail.

Embrace the icebound beauty,
Feel the chill, hold it near,
In these celestial hues we find,
A universe crystal clear.

Celestial Dancers on Frozen Ground

Under the moon's silver glow,
Stars twirl like whispers on air.
Frost-kissed breezes softly flow,
Nature's waltz, a gentle affair.

Sparks of light in the dark ocean,
Each flicker a silent song.
Awakening deep emotion,
As night dances, we belong.

Through frozen fields, shadows glide,
Veils of mist caress the trees.
In the stillness, dreams confide,
To the rhythm of the freeze.

Wish upon these glowing lights,
Let your heart take flight, ignite.
In the hush of frosty nights,
Celestial dancers, pure delight.

Crystals form on ancient ground,
Memories caught in time’s embrace.
In this beauty, silence found,
Forever held in winter’s grace.

Glaciers of Time in a Soft Embrace

Frozen giants slowly shift,
Holding stories in their weight.
Time, a gift, a gentle rift,
Layers thick with years create.

Ripples glisten, ages pass,
Echoes of the earth's deep sighs.
In their depth, reflections glass,
Secrets held beneath the skies.

Cool winds whisper ancient truths,
Carving paths through icy veins.
Nature's art, a dance of youth,
Molding beauty from the pains.

As the world around them sleeps,
Glaciers guard the silent past.
In their silence, wisdom keeps,
A testament to time steadfast.

In the twilight, shadows play,
Glimmers of the ages spun.
Caught in silence, night and day,
Glaciers hold what's never done.

Crystalline Poetry of the Night

Stars like crystals, bright and clear,
Whispers of light in midnight's hand.
Each twinkle, a memory dear,
Written in an endless strand.

Moonlight spills on silver streams,
Shimmering paths where dreams reside.
Nature hums its gentle themes,
In this symphony, we confide.

The night air carries secrets low,
In the hush of whispered lore.
Crystalline visions softly flow,
Opening every unseen door.

In the stillness, hearts entwine,
With the cosmos, we connect.
Lines of beauty, fate divine,
In the night, we introspect.

Wrapped in velvet, shadows blend,
Where silence dances, thoughts can soar.
In the dark, we find our friend,
Crystalline poetry evermore.

Reflections of Brightness on Cold Skin

Morning light breaks through the gloom,
Kissing frost from winter's breath.
Each ray a promise, a bloom,
Awakening life from quiet death.

Brightness twinkles on snow's crest,
Like diamonds scattered, pure and bright.
In these moments, hearts find rest,
As the day conquers the night.

Cold air bites, yet warmth appears,
In the dance of sun and frost.
Nature's beauty draws us near,
In the glow of what was lost.

Each reflection tells a tale,
Of resilience in the face of strife.
In the shimmer, we prevail,
Finding joy in fleeting life.

Embrace the warmth that challenges cold,
As sunlight weaves through winter's thread.
A tapestry of stories told,
Reflections on skin, hope widespread.

A Journey Through Frosted Bliss

Through the fields where snowflakes dance,
Whispers of winter in a trance.
Softly falling, a blanket of white,
Embracing the earth with pure delight.

Footprints marked in frosted ground,
Secrets of nature softly found.
Each step taken, a moment to freeze,
In this wonderland, calm and at ease.

Glistening trees in the pale moonlight,
Shimmering branches, a magical sight.
Beneath the stars, the world feels new,
A journey unfolds, ever so true.

Laughter echoes through the chill air,
As joyful hearts venture with care.
With every breath, a cloud of white,
Together we wander through the night.

In this realm of crisp, frosted bliss,
We find a joy we dare not miss.
Embracing the chill, we forge ahead,
Onward we go, where dreams are fed.

Glistening Threads of Nightfall Joy

Crimson skies meet twilight's embrace,
A tapestry woven in time and space.
Stars awaken with a shimmering wink,
In this moment, we pause to think.

Moonlight threads through the trees so tall,
Casting shadows, a soft, silver thrall.
Nature whispers secrets, old and wise,
As the night unveils its gentle guise.

Breezes carry the scent of pine,
Filling the air with joy divine.
Laughter echoes, hearts intertwine,
In this realm where souls align.

With every step on the cool, soft ground,
Magic lingers, endlessly found.
The night unfolds, glowing bright,
As we wander through the starlit night.

Joy dances lightly on the breeze,
In glistening threads, our hearts find ease.
Together, we cherish the night's sweet grace,
In the warmth of love, we find our place.

Silence Wrapped in Icicle Tapestry

In the hush of winter's breath,
Nature's beauty whispers, rebirth from death.
Icicles hang like delicate art,
Each one a masterpiece, set apart.

The world lies still, a soft, white sheen,
Wrapped in silence, tranquil and serene.
Trees draped in frost, a magical sight,
In this breathtaking scene, hearts take flight.

Footsteps muffled on the icy floor,
Every sound echoes, a calming roar.
Time stands still, as shadows play,
In this frozen dream, we drift away.

Clarity found in the cold embrace,
Each moment savored, a gentle grace.
Silence wraps around with tender care,
In this icicle tapestry, we bare.

Breath of the winter, crisp and bright,
Illuminating paths in the still night.
With every heartbeat, a sacred kiss,
In this stillness, we find our bliss.

Crystalline Hues at Dusk's Call

As the sun dips low, the colors blend,
Crystalline hues gently descend.
Soft pastels kiss the twilight sky,
In beauty’s embrace, we breathe a sigh.

The horizon glows, a painter's delight,
Blushing shades of gold and light.
With every moment, we chase the dusk,
Fragrant whispers, nature's husk.

Stars peek out, shy and rare,
Twinkling secrets float in the air.
Each shimmering light, a wish to share,
In this evening's embrace, we find care.

The world transforms in twilight's grace,
Each breath a promise, each glance a trace.
Chasing shadows in the fading sun,
In crystalline hues, we are one.

Nightfall whispers, bidding adieu,
As dreams awaken with night’s debut.
In the tapestry woven by dusk's call,
We find ourselves, we find it all.

Whispers of Frost-kissed Dreams

In the quiet night, dreams unfold,
Frosty whispers, tales untold,
Stars twinkle softly, casting light,
Chilling secrets, veiled in white.

Snowflakes dance, gentle and free,
Carpet of white, a serene spree,
Each breath a cloud, crisp and bright,
Wrapped in wonder, pure delight.

Moonlit shadows softly creep,
Awakening visions from deep,
Nature's hush, a soothing balm,
In icy stillness, the world feels calm.

Nightingale's song, tender and clear,
Guides the wanderer's heart near,
Every flake a wish, a dream,
Beneath the stars, all thoughts gleam.

With the dawn, colors will beam,
Yet until then, we'll softly dream,
In the heart of frost, we find our way,
Through whispers of night, we gently sway.

Luminescent Winter Serenade

Underneath the silver glow,
Winter's song begins to flow,
Softly echoing through the air,
A serenade, pure and rare.

Frosted trees, aglow with light,
Whispers of snowflakes take flight,
Every note a crystal chime,
Harmony flows, marking time.

Echoes dance upon the wind,
Carried dreams, a tale to send,
In the stillness, hearts ignite,
Music weaves the winter's night.

Stars like diamonds in the sky,
Glistening gems that float on high,
Nature’s orchestration, deep and wide,
In this magic, we find our guide.

As twilight fades to morning’s grace,
Winter’s song leaves a soft trace,
In each breath, a world we share,
Luminescent dreams are everywhere.

Embrace of the Silent Flakes

Gentle touch upon the ground,
Silent flakes, without a sound,
They weave a quilt from skies above,
An embrace of winter's love.

Each flake unique, sculpted with care,
Adorning rooftops, trees laid bare,
Whispers of nature softly fall,
A tender blanket, covering all.

In the crisp air, laughter rings,
Children play as joy takes wings,
In every swirl, the world feels bright,
In this embrace, hearts take flight.

Candles flicker, warm and glow,
Through the windows, soft light flows,
In this haven, peace does grow,
As silent flakes continue to show.

With every sunset’s golden hue,
The world transforms, fresh and new,
An invitation to step outside,
In the embrace, let joy abide.

Shimmers on the Frozen Surface

Glints upon the frozen lake,
Reflecting dreams, paths we make,
Whispers of ice, secrets to find,
In the stillness, hearts unwind.

The world a canvas, white and bright,
Every shimmer, a spark of light,
Underneath, the stories flow,
Beneath the surface, life will grow.

Footsteps crunch in rhythmic song,
In this quiet, we belong,
Nature's splendor, pure and true,
In each moment, a world anew.

Moonlight dances on the waves,
In the night, the spirit braves,
With each glisten, time stands still,
Caught in wonder, hearts will thrill.

As dawn approaches, colors rise,
Breaking through the still, dark skies,
In the shimmer of the day,
Frozen beauty lights the way.

Secrets of the Winter Night

Whispers of snow softly fall,
Cloaking the earth in a white shawl.
Stars twinkle in the velvet space,
Mysteries held in each frosty trace.

Moonlight dances on frozen streams,
Echoes of long-forgotten dreams.
Silent stories the night bestows,
Wrapped in warmth as the cold wind blows.

Footsteps crunch on the icy ground,
In this stillness, peace is found.
Shadows flicker like lantern light,
Guiding hearts through the winter night.

Breath hangs like clouds in the air,
Hopeful wishes rise without a care.
Magic lives in the frigid breeze,
Secrets whispered among the trees.

Nature sleeps under a soft quilt,
In these moments, calm is built.
Stars above keep watchful eyes,
Guarding the dreams that softly rise.

Embracing the Chill of Solitude

Alone beneath the starry sky,
I find solace, just me and the night.
The chill wraps round like a gentle shawl,
In silence, I embrace it all.

No voices break the tranquil air,
Just the sound of frost everywhere.
Each breath a cloud, so light, so free,
In solitude, I come to be.

Crimson sunsets fade into gloom,
As twilight dances to the moon's tune.
With every shadow that stretches long,
I find a sense of being strong.

The cold bites, yet I feel alive,
In this peace, my spirit can thrive.
Winter's chill may numb the skin,
But it awakens the warmth within.

Here in the stillness, I stand tall,
Embracing the quiet that binds us all.
A heart at peace, a soul untamed,
In the solitude, I'm still unashamed.

Frosty Murmurs in the Stillness

In the hush of the wintry night,
Soft murmurs dance in silver light.
The world outside, a frozen glow,
Cradled gently by the flurries' flow.

Branches bow under the weight,
Whispers of snow, a silent fate.
Every flake tells its own tale,
In this stillness, dreams set sail.

Stars shine like diamonds, bold and bright,
A testament to the tranquil night.
Moments stretch as time stands still,
In this peace, I savor the chill.

A world wrapped in a frosty embrace,
Finding warmth in nature's grace.
Each breath a cloud, each heartbeat clear,
In winter's arms, I have no fear.

Murmurs fade into the dawn's light,
Promise of warmth after this night.
Yet the magic of frosty air,
Lingers softly, everywhere.

Ethereal Embrace of the Cold Night

Underneath the starry expanse,
The winter night unfolds its dance.
An ethereal touch, so crisp and bright,
Whispers secrets in the soft twilight.

Each breath of air a frozen spark,
Painting dreams in the shadows dark.
The stillness wraps like a gentle embrace,
In the cold night, I find my place.

Snowflakes twirl in their silent flight,
Glittering like jewels in the night.
An orchestra of winter's sweet song,
In this moment, I know I belong.

The moon's glow bathes the world anew,
Illuminating paths for those who pursue.
A heart aligned with nature's tune,
Dwells in the magic of the moon's rune.

In the chill, my spirit soars,
Finding peace through winter's doors.
The night, a canvas of dreams untold,
In its embrace, I am bold.

Chill of the Ether's Luminescence

In shadows cast by silver light,
The chill wraps round, compact and tight.
Whispers dance on icy air,
A frozen dream, a magic rare.

Glistening stars in velvet skies,
Awake the night with breathless sighs.
Each flicker speaks of secrets deep,
In the stillness, none shall sleep.

Through the pines, a howl does creep,
Echoes 'neath the frost-kissed sweep.
Nature breathes in quiet tune,
Wrapped tightly in the cold of June.

A spellbound world in twilight's grasp,
Time shatters with an icy clasp.
Moments linger, soft and pale,
In the ether where dreams prevail.

The Stillness of a White Embrace

A world adorned in blankets white,
Softly whispers, heart takes flight.
Nature pauses, takes a breath,
In this stillness, finds no death.

Pines whisper secrets in the frost,
In this still embrace, all is lost.
Time stands still, a frozen sigh,
As soft flakes tumble from the sky.

Beneath the weight of winter's quilt,
A vision born from nature's lilt.
The quietude wraps close and near,
In every heart, a whisper clear.

A moment held, forever bright,
In the calm of soft moonlight.
All is hushed, the world at peace,
In winter's clutch, sweet thoughts increase.

Twinkling Stars in a Frosted Canopy

Underneath the frosted dome,
Twinkling stars find a quiet home.
Each glimmer tells a tale untold,
In the embrace of night so cold.

Whispers of the winds traverse,
As frosted branches gently converse.
The sky wears diamonds, pure and bright,
Painting dreams in the depth of night.

Moonbeams dance on blankets white,
Inviting dreams to take their flight.
A world where silence reigns supreme,
In the frost, we weave our dream.

Upon the earth, where shadows play,
A tender night awaits the day.
In this stillness, hearts align,
In the frost, the stars entwine.

Serendipity Under the Icicle Moon

Beneath the heavy icicle glow,
Paths converge where soft winds blow.
In frozen whispers, fate aligned,
A serendipitous love designed.

Crystals hang from branches bare,
Each glint reflects a secret flair.
Moments linger, sweet and shy,
As pale lights twinkle in the sky.

Frosted breath on winter's face,
A dance unfolds of fragile grace.
The world aglow with tender charms,
Wrapped closely in each other's arms.

Underneath this icy spell,
Where hearts entwined do gently dwell.
In this silence, love finds its tune,
Forever wed to the icicle moon.

Kaleidoscope of Frozen Dreams

Glistening flakes in twilight's glow,
Painting paths where soft winds blow.
Whispers dance beneath the trees,
A tapestry of cold memories.

Reflections sparkle, colors blend,
In each turn, new tales suspend.
Frigid hues in twilight's gleam,
Life unfolds in winter's dream.

Silent laughter fills the air,
Frosty air, yet hearts laid bare.
Every crystal tells a story,
Of fleeting moments, lost in glory.

Moonlight our gentle guide tonight,
Casting shadows, soft and bright.
With each sigh, the echoes claim,
A canvas born from winter’s name.

In this world of swirling light,
We chase the dreams that take to flight.
Kaleidoscope of time and space,
Held within winter's warm embrace.

Shelter in a Winter’s Embrace

Beneath the blanket of soft white,
We find our solace, pure delight.
The world outside, a chilling breeze,
Yet here, our hearts are free to tease.

Fires crackle with tales untold,
In every flicker, warmth unfolds.
Windows framed with glistening frost,
In this haven, we count no cost.

Woolen blankets piled high and snug,
Laughter dances, warm and snug.
Cocoa steaming, candles bright,
Wrapped in magic of the night.

Snowflakes swirl, a gentle dance,
Outside, the world in winter's trance.
Yet here within, we softly smile,
In love's embrace, we'll stay a while.

Together in this winter's dawn,
In shadows cast, our fears are gone.
For in the chill, we come alive,
Sheltered close, our hearts will thrive.

Frost-kissed Echoes of Affection

Frost-kissed whispers touch the air,
Where love resides, so pure, so rare.
Tender moments carved in time,
Each heartbeat sings a silent rhyme.

The world, a canvas painted white,
Echoes of laughter, pure delight.
Snowflakes landing on your face,
In this chill, I find my place.

Hand in hand, we wander slow,
Through silver fields where wild winds blow.
Every step a promise made,
With every flake, our fears do fade.

As twilight paints the skies aglow,
We share our secrets, soft and low.
In frozen whispers, love is clear,
In every heartbeat, you are near.

Frost-kissed dreams linger in sight,
Those echoes shimmer in the night.
In every flake, our hearts align,
Forever wrapped in love divine.

Enchantment of the Winter Sun

Golden rays through branches weave,
A winter's morn, so hard to leave.
Frost still clings to every leaf,
Yet warmth awakens, fierce belief.

Pine-scented air fills the lane,
Chasing shadows, easing pain.
Each beam whispers in the still,
A promise made, a heartfelt thrill.

Ice crystals sparkle, catch the light,
Turning gray to purest white.
Nature wears her diamond crown,
In this magic, never down.

As snowdrops bloom beneath the cold,
In their beauty, tales unfold.
With every dawn, a fresh embrace,
The winter sun restores our grace.

Together we bask in morning's glow,
Finding warmth where cold winds blow.
In the heart of winter's reign,
We find our joy, we break the chain.

Frosted Hearts in Evening Glow

In twilight's hush, the shadows play,
Soft whispers of the end of day.
A frosted touch upon the ground,
Hearts awaken to the silent sound.

Stars begin their twinkling dance,
Frosted hearts in a mesmerizing trance.
Breath like smoke in the winter's grip,
Each moment savored, a gentle sip.

The moon casts silver on trees so bare,
A tranquil promise hangs in the air.
Together under this tranquil sky,
With frosted hearts, we stand, not shy.

Dreams take flight on this chilly night,
Wrapped in warmth, held tight, just right.
Frosted patterns in the air we trace,
In evening glow, we find our place.

Together we'll weave these moments dear,
Frosted hearts without a fear.
In this embrace, let shadows fall,
Evening glow, our one true call.

Dances Beneath the Winter Glow

Beneath the stars, the night does sing,
Winter's breath brings a delicate wing.
Dances under the lunar light,
Hearts entwined, holding on tight.

The frost creates a shimmering scene,
As shadows play, so soft and serene.
Twinkling skies mirror our joy,
In this moment, nothing can destroy.

Swaying gently, like trees in the breeze,
Every movement aims to please.
Snowflakes sparkle, a magical sight,
In our dance, the world feels right.

Around us, whispers of love abound,
In the air, such beauty is found.
With every twirl, the night ignites,
Beneath the winter, our hearts take flight.

Forever treasured, this night will stay,
In memories spun from purest play.
Dances beneath the frosty glow,
A timeless love, forever flows.

Twilight Chandeliers of Ice

In the dusk's embrace, ice chandeliers shine,
Each crystal dangling, a work so divine.
As evening falls, they catch the light,
Twilight whispers, a magical sight.

Flickering stars in a velvet sky,
Under the gaze of the moon up high.
Reflections dance on a frozen lake,
Creating a world that dreams can make.

Gentle breezes carry soft sighs,
While shimmering beauty never lies.
Ice sculptures stand in nature's art,
Each piece crafted by a winter's heart.

A hush surrounds, as the night unfolds,
The frozen tales of ancients told.
Chandeliers twinkle like secrets shared,
In twilight's glow, with love declared.

Hold my hand as we wander through,
This crystal world, just me and you.
Twilight chandeliers weave a story,
In ice and light, we find our glory.

Echoes of a Crystal Embrace

An echo calls through the silent night,
A crystal embrace that feels so right.
In shadows deep, we find our way,
Through whispers soft, where dreams hold sway.

The moonlight dances on a frozen stream,
Reflecting hopes, the sweetest dream.
In this moment, time stands still,
Hearts connected by a gentle thrill.

Snowflakes fall like whispered prayers,
Each one carries love, unspoken cares.
In the quiet, a bond is found,
Echoes linger, they swirl around.

Wrapped in warmth against the chill,
With every heartbeat, we feel the thrill.
Crystal embrace, a promise made,
In the silence, our fears allayed.

Together we'll roam through starry skies,
With echoes of love that never die.
In this embrace, forever stay,
A crystal night, where dreams play.

Starlit Paths on Frozen Ground

Beneath the sky so vast and bright,
Footsteps crunch on silvered night.
Whispers of dreams begin to flow,
Each step a tale from long ago.

The air is crisp, the world aglow,
With every star, new hopes bestow.
Frozen trails where echoes sing,
A symphony that winter brings.

Shadows dance on diamond frost,
In this expanse, no joy is lost.
The moonlight paints the trees so tall,
While serenity wraps around all.

Night's embrace, a tender wrap,
Nature sighs, a gentle nap.
Time slows down in this friendly hold,
As stories weave through paths of cold.

With each breath, a dream unfurls,
In the stillness where magic twirls.
Starlit paths, a journey found,
In frozen realms, our hearts unbound.

Lucent Crystals Singing Softly

Under the trees, the crystals gleam,
Reflecting each light like a dream.
Silent songs in the frosty air,
Nature's whispers, gentle and rare.

Icicles dangle like fragile notes,
Each one tells what winter promotes.
In every shimmer, a story spun,
A dance of beauty has just begun.

Beneath the weight of frozen grace,
Every crystal finds its place.
Harmony swells in the still of night,
As stars embrace with radiant light.

The ground adorned with sparkling lace,
A wintry quilt, a soft embrace.
As darkness falls, the beauty speaks,
In every shimmer, the heart seeks.

Lucent echoes of frost divine,
In every glimmer, hearts entwine.
A world transformed, a fairy’s song,
In this crystal realm, we belong.

Moonbeams Dancing on Expanses Cold

Moonlight drapes the world in silver,
With each ray, the shadows quiver.
Silent night, the whispers call,
While silver paths invite us all.

Dancing beams on winter's skin,
A gentle glow from deep within.
Footprints soft on powdered snow,
Each step leads where dreams may flow.

The night unfurls its vast embrace,
As moonbeams trace a tender place.
Magic sleeps in the frosty air,
Wrapped in dreams beyond compare.

In the stillness, secrets hide,
While shimmering wonders coincide.
The cold may freeze, but hearts ignite,
As moonbeams waltz through the mystic night.

Blankets of stars, a lustrous choir,
Wrapping the world in warm desire.
Here in the night, with spirits bold,
We dance with the moon on expanses cold.

Shrouded in Winter's Gentle Whisper

Wrapped in blankets of softest white,
A hush descends, the world feels right.
Winter drapes its calming hand,
In this serene, enchanted land.

Crisp air fills the spaces near,
Every heartbeat, crystal clear.
Through wooded trails where silence reigns,
The gentle whisper eases pains.

Snowflakes swirl like fleeting thoughts,
In nature's grip, the spirit knots.
Still moments wrapped in winter's grace,
Time stands still, no need to race.

Beneath the boughs, where shadows play,
Memories linger, softly sway.
Hope unfurls in every flake,
As winter's breath begins to wake.

A cozy warmth in each cold glance,
Brings forth the heart in quiet dance.
Shrouded in whispers, tender and light,
We find our peace on this winter night.

Glacial Grace and Warmth Within

In the stillness of a winter's night,
Whispers danced with quiet light.
Graceful forms of ice and snow,
Hidden warmth begins to glow.

Beneath the cold, a heart beats clear,
Fires igniting, drawing near.
Nature's hush, a peaceful sigh,
Glacial grace beneath the sky.

Crystal shadows softly play,
Dreams emerge and drift away.
In this chill, a spark is born,
Of tender love, a new day sworn.

Frosty branches arch in glee,
While warmth wraps around like a plea.
Holding close the fragile thread,
Where glacial grace is gently spread.

In the landscape pure and white,
Hope ignites in the quiet night.
With every breath, a promise shines,
A dance of warmth, in cold confines.

Dreams Encased in Frosted Linger

Caught beneath a frosted veil,
Dreams unfold like ships that sail.
Wrapped in whispers, soft and bright,
Nighttime calls with shimmering light.

Frozen echoes charm the air,
Haunting thoughts, a bold affair.
In the silence, wishes thrive,
Encased in frost, they come alive.

Sparkling dreams in cold embrace,
Chasing shadows, finding grace.
Held by winter's gentle touch,
Frozen hopes that mean so much.

With each breath of icy air,
Moments linger, tender care.
Beauty blooms in chilly skies,
Frosted lingers, where love lies.

Every star a wishful gleam,
Embraced within a crystal dream.
In the quiet, hearts are stirred,
As magic weaves the softest words.

Serenity Stitched in Crystal Threads

In the calm of a snowy eve,
Crystal threads begin to weave.
Patterns form with gentle grace,
Serenity in every space.

Nature’s quilt drapes softly down,
A tapestry in white and brown.
Each thread speaks a silent lore,
Of peaceful moments, evermore.

Beneath the frost, the world stands still,
Time suspended on winter's hill.
Gentle strokes of icy breath,
Life entwined in love and death.

Whispers flow like rivers clear,
Echoes of what we hold dear.
Stitched in harmony, hearts align,
In crystal bonds, a love divine.

Through the dusky, chill embrace,
Warmth emerges, fills the space.
In serenity, we find our way,
Guided softly, night and day.

Luminous Frost and Heartfelt Melodies

Underneath the moon's soft glow,
Luminous frost begins to flow.
Heartfelt melodies drift and sway,
In the night's embrace, we stay.

Every flake a note in time,
Played with care, a sweet rhyme.
Winter's breath, a gentle song,
Weaving tales where we belong.

With each step, the world ignites,
Magic twinkles, pure delights.
In the silence, dreams are spun,
Frosty whispers, a new day's sun.

Through the night, our spirits glide,
In warm embraces, side by side.
Heartfelt echoes fill the air,
Luminous frost, beyond compare.

As dawn breaks, the chill recedes,
Melodies turn into seeds.
In the light, our love will soar,
Frosty dreams forevermore.

Echoes of Joy in Winter’s Silence

In the hush of falling snow,
Whispers of laughter flow.
Children's voices, soft and bright,
Echo through the joyful night.

Candles flicker, warm and gold,
Tales of wonder, stories told.
Hearts unite in cozy cheer,
Through the chill, love draws us near.

Footprints traced in purest white,
Mark our paths with sheer delight.
Hand in hand, we roam and play,
In the heart of winter's sway.

The silence sings a gentle song,
Where we gather, we belong.
In this moment, peace confides,
Echoes of joy in winter's strides.

As stars twinkle, dreams unfold,
In the warmth, our hopes hold.
Every breath a treasure shared,
In the silence, we are spared.

A Dance of Shadows in the Winter Light

Underneath the silver moon,
Shadows dance, a gentle tune.
Nighttime whispers, soft and low,
In the winter's quiet glow.

Footprints fade as silence breaks,
In the stillness, magic wakes.
Frosty air and hearts ignite,
With the dance of winter light.

Branches bare, yet spirits soar,
Moonlit paths invite for more.
In the chill, we move as one,
Chasing shadows, we have fun.

Echoes linger, sweet embrace,
In the night, we find our place.
Every twirl and every sway,
Guides our hearts till break of day.

As the dawn begins to rise,
Colors bloom in winter skies.
In that moment, such delight,
A dance of shadows, pure and bright.

Frosty Teardrops of Enchanted Joy

Frosty teardrops glisten bright,
Underneath the pale moonlight.
Each one tells a tale anew,
Of the beauty that we view.

In the stillness, magic lies,
Whispering in winter skies.
Every flake, a story shared,
In the joy, we are prepared.

As the world transforms to white,
Hearts awaken, pure delight.
In the cold, we gather close,
Chasing dreams that matter most.

Sparkling jewels on branches sway,
Fleeting moments of the day.
With each breath, our spirits soar,
Frosty teardrops, evermore.

In the warming light we find,
All the love that binds us kind.
With hearts open, we embrace,
Frosty teardrops, joy’s sweet grace.

Beneath a Blanket of Purest White

Beneath a blanket, soft and white,
Rest the dreams of day and night.
Winter whispers, secrets told,
In the hush, warmth to behold.

Each flake falls like quiet grace,
Wrapping all in a soft embrace.
Hushed are sounds, the world is still,
In this peace, hearts gently thrill.

Sunrise glimmers on the snow,
Filling every heart with glow.
In the crystal, magic grows,
Underneath, love softly flows.

With our laughter, skies ignite,
Colors shimmer, pure delight.
Under blankets, dreams take flight,
Creating joy in winter's light.

As the season softly sighs,
In this quiet, our spirits rise.
Beneath a blanket, side by side,
Together in the winter’s ride.

A Canvas of Night's Frosted Art

In the hush of the silent night,
Stars twinkle like diamonds bright.
Moonlight spills on the frozen ground,
Whispers of magic all around.

Frost paints the leaves in silver hue,
Each breath puffs clouds, a frosty view.
Shadows dance in the cool, crisp air,
A tapestry woven with delicate care.

Breezes carry secrets unseen,
Glistening dreams in the moonbeam.
Nature’s palette, a vision rare,
A canvas of night beyond compare.

Shining Gifts of a Frigid Dawn

Morning breaks with a gentle sigh,
Painting the sky with a soft, warm cry.
Crystals sparkle, the world aglow,
Gifts of winter in the sun’s warm flow.

Trees stand tall, cloaked in white,
A breathtaking view, a lovely sight.
Pine boughs bend with a frosty crest,
Nature awakens, a soothing rest.

Birds take flight, a joyful dance,
In the chill, they twirl and prance.
Each note sung is a melody sweet,
Celebrating life in the morning's greet.

Veins of Ice and Light's Embrace

Rivers freeze in the grasp of night,
Mirrors reflecting the pale moonlight.
Cracked earth rests beneath a sheet,
Veins of ice, where silence meets.

Glacial whispers echo low,
Stories of nature's ancient flow.
Among the stillness, a heartbeat strong,
In the dance of winter, we belong.

Colors muted, but beauty thrives,
In frosted realms, the spirit strives.
Ice and light in a warm embrace,
Nature's tranquil, timeless grace.

Timeless Beauty in Winter's Grasp

Underneath a blanket of snow,
The earth is hushed, its secrets slow.
Every flake a story to tell,
In winter's grip, all is well.

Footprints mark a fleeting past,
Wanderers roam, their shadows cast.
Whispers of winds, a distant song,
In this stillness, we all belong.

Sparkling frost on branches sway,
A world transformed, in shades of gray.
Timeless beauty, forever near,
In every heartbeat, winter clear.

Twilight's Shimmering Cascade

As daylight fades to softest hue,
The stars emerge from skies of blue.
Whispers of night begin to gleam,
In twilight's hush, we start to dream.

Reflections dance on waters still,
Night's gentle hand brings forth the thrill.
The moonbeams bathe the earth in light,
As shadows play, embracing night.

Each moment holds a touch divine,
A canvas where our hopes align.
Beyond the veil, the dreams take flight,
In twilight's arms, we find delight.

The breeze carries a sweet embrace,
While nature weaves its magic lace.
Together lost in this embrace,
We trace the stars, our secret place.

Amidst the glow of evening's grace,
We find our hearts, a shared space.
In twilight's shimmer, dreams cascade,
Forever in this night we've made.

Cuddle in the Winter's Breath

The world outside is cold and bright,
Wrapped in white, a wondrous sight.
We draw together, warmth we share,
In winter’s breath, the frosty air.

Through frosted glass, the world appears,
A soft retreat from melting fears.
The fire crackles, embers glow,
With every moment, love will grow.

Amid the chill, our hearts ignite,
In shared reprieve from winter’s bite.
You lean in close, a gentle sigh,
In cozy comfort, time goes by.

Snowflakes dance on softest breeze,
While whispers blend with rustling leaves.
Together in this snowy nest,
A cuddle close, we find our rest.

When morning breaks with golden hue,
We'll face the day, just me and you.
For in this winter's tender breath,
We find the warmth that conquers death.

Echoes Beneath the Winter Sky

The quiet falls, the world sleeps tight,
Beneath the glow of silver light.
Each flake that falls, a soft refrain,
In this stillness, whispers wane.

Branches bare and frosty cold,
Stories of the night unfold.
Echoes of laughter fill the air,
In winter's grasp, we pause and stare.

Reflections deep in icy streams,
The night unveils our heartfelt dreams.
With every breath, a crystalline sigh,
Together we stand 'neath winter's sky.

The stars above begin to weave,
A tapestry of night, believe.
In chilly air, our voices blend,
With every note, the shadows mend.

In silence, secrets softly roam,
Beneath the sky, we find our home.
In echoes shared, our hearts soar high,
Connected strong, beneath the sky.

Glimmers of a Snow-Kissed World

In morning light, the snowflakes gleam,
A wonderland, a perfect dream.
Each step we take, a crunch of snow,
In nature's arms, our spirits glow.

The trees adorned with frosty lace,
A magical and sacred space.
As laughter rings through frozen air,
In every flake, a moment rare.

With every turn, the world awakes,
A canvas bright, where beauty makes.
The glimmering path ahead unfolds,
A tale of warmth, in winter's hold.

Together lost in this sweet bliss,
We share a world not one could miss.
With hearts entwined, we roam and twirl,
In glimmers of a snow-kissed world.

The sun will rise, the day will call,
But in this realm, we'll have it all.
For in the snow, our dreams we find,
In every glimmer, love entwined.

Serenade of the Silent Night

In the hush of evening's glow,
Stars above begin to show.
Whispers soft and dreams take flight,
Wrapped in peace, the silent night.

Beneath the moon, the shadows dance,
Nature sways in sweet romance.
Melodies of dreams unfold,
In the night, their tales are told.

Lunar light on glistening snow,
Time stands still, the world aglow.
Each heartbeat blends with winter's song,
In this silence, we belong.

Faint echoes drift through frosty air,
Crystals gleam, a beauty rare.
In the stillness, hearts unite,
Lost in dreams of the night.

So let us cherish every sigh,
Underneath the velvet sky.
In the serenade of stars so bright,
We find our peace in silent night.

Icicle Dreams and Warmth

Hanging clear like fragile glass,
Icicles shimmer, moments pass.
Dreams weave in the frosty air,
A whispered wish, beyond all care.

Fires crackle, warmth within,
Against the chill where feelings begin.
Gathered close, stories we share,
Moments treasured, beyond compare.

Snowflakes drift on winter's breath,
Softly falling, a dance with death.
Yet in this frigid beauty found,
Hope ignites, all around.

Every sparkle tells a tale,
Of journeys taken, love's prevail.
Icicle dreams in warm embrace,
Whispered joys that time can't erase.

Underneath the starry haze,
We hold tight to cherished ways.
Icicles gleam, yet heartbeats soar,
In winter's chill, we long for more.

Moonlit Crystals on Frozen Ground

Moonlight dances on frozen streams,
Casting shadows, igniting dreams.
Crystals sparkle, pure and bright,
A canvas painted by the night.

Whispers float on the winter breeze,
Embracing silence among the trees.
Nature's art, a wondrous sight,
Wrapped in soft, celestial light.

Each step crunches on the frosted floor,
Echoes linger, forevermore.
Underneath the starry crown,
The beauty rests, without a frown.

Frosted breath and winter's chill,
In this moment, the heart stands still.
Moonlit pathways wait to be walked,
In the night, where dreams are talked.

Crystals fade with the break of dawn,
Yet memories linger, softly drawn.
Frozen moments, forever found,
In moonlit crystals on frozen ground.

Embrace of the Frosted Dawn

A gentle glow breaks through the night,
Awakening the world in light.
Frosted hues embrace the trees,
Dewdrops glimmer, kissed by breeze.

Softly sighs the waking earth,
In every shadow, there's new birth.
Birds take flight, their songs resound,
In the embrace of dawn unbound.

Whispers linger in the air,
Moments wrapped in beauty rare.
Colors splashed on canvas wide,
In frost's embrace, we all confide.

Morning breaks with tender grace,
Chasing shadows from their place.
Hope ignites as the sun draws near,
In frosted dawn, our hearts adhere.

So let us greet this day anew,
With every breath, a chance to pursue.
In the dawn's embrace, we find our way,
With love and light, come what may.

Frosted Petals in Starlit Silence

In the quiet of the night,
Frosted petals softly gleam,
Whispers of a chill delight,
In the moonlight's gentle dream.

Silence drapes the frozen ground,
A hushed breath within the cold,
Nature's beauty all around,
Stories of the night unfold.

Stars like diamonds spark the dark,
Lights that twinkle, fade, and sway,
While the world lies still and stark,
In this night's embrace, we stay.

Petals kissed by frost's soft hand,
Crystals glisten in the light,
A frozen beauty, pure and grand,
Caught within the breath of night.

Winter wraps the earth in peace,
As time slows beneath the glow,
In this hush, our worries cease,
Frosted dreams begin to flow.

Chilled Reverie of the Heart

In the corners of the mind,
Chilled whispers gently sing,
Memories of love entwined,
With the frost, they take to wing.

Echoes of a tender past,
In the chill, they softly bloom,
Like the shadows they are cast,
In the quiet room's cold gloom.

Hearts that beat in winter's grasp,
Palms held close, a tender choice,
In the stillness, dare to clasp,
Hear the frozen, silent voice.

Each breath forms a crystal hue,
As the world lies still in dreams,
Chilled reveries seep anew,
Through the night, a whisper beams.

Beneath the stars, our spirits rise,
In the cold, our warmth ignites,
And in this spell, our love replies,
As the heart's chill softly lights.

Dance of the Winter Whispers

Softly falls the morning frost,
While the trees in stillness sway,
Winter’s breath, a line embossed,
In the night that fades away.

Whispers dance on winds so light,
Glistening upon the ground,
Nature’s song in purest flight,
In the silence, love is found.

Eager footsteps mark the way,
In the snow, dreams intertwine,
Clouds above begin to play,
As the sun begins to shine.

With each flake, a tale unfolds,
In harmony with time's own art,
Winter's whispers softly hold,
As we twirl, a swaying heart.

Together in this frozen world,
Where each breath becomes a song,
In this dance, dreams are unfurled,
In winter's grasp, where we belong.

Silver Raindrops on Crystal Limbs

Silver raindrops softly fall,
Kissing limbs of crystal trees,
Nature’s dance, a calming thrall,
Echoing through winter's breeze.

Every drop a fleeting glance,
In the shimmer of the night,
A submission to the chance,
To become part of the light.

Branches sway, a graceful sigh,
Held in liquid silver's clasp,
As the world breathes, we comply,
In nature's tender, soft grasp.

With each fall, the silence speaks,
Whispers of the heart's desire,
In the quiet, warmth still seeks,
Faced with winter's frosty fire.

In this moment, lost in time,
Raindrops dance a hidden tune,
A spark in the cold, sublime,
Beneath the watchful, glimmering moon.

Radiance Encased in Winter's Hold

In frosted air, the stillness hums,
Crystals cling to trees like songs.
A silver glow on icy blooms,
Silent whispers, nature longs.

Every breath, a cloud of dreams,
Stars shine bright in velvet skies.
Warmth encased in winter's beams,
Hope unfurls as daylight sighs.

Hidden sparks in winter's chill,
Time stands still, yet time will flow.
In frigid realms, a heart can thrill,
For beauty lies where cold winds blow.

Through muted shades, the colors rise,
Life persists beneath the frost.
Radiance lives, it never dies,
In winter's hold, not all is lost.

A Symphony of Shadows in Freeze

Beneath the hush of winter's breath,
Shadows dance with graceful ease.
In the chill, we find the depth,
Melodies that tease the trees.

Frosted fingers touch the night,
Echoes born in silver light.
Silent notes, a sweet delight,
Wrapped in whispers, soft and bright.

Crimson skies at break of dawn,
Nature's lullaby unfolds.
In the dusk, a world reborn,
Every shadow, a tale told.

Harmony within the cold,
Each heartbeat beats a steady rhyme.
A symphony, brave and bold,
In frozen spaces, we find time.

Shining Spirits in the Winter's Grasp

In the twilight, spirits glow,
Beneath the stars, a silver line.
Winter’s grasp may seem so slow,
Yet light breaks through, forever fine.

Boughs adorned with icy lace,
Every moment, magic swells.
In this realm, we find our place,
Where warmth within the silence dwells.

Flakes of snow, like wishes cast,
Carried on the show of night.
Memories of seasons past,
In the cold, our dreams take flight.

Hope ignites in darkest hours,
Beneath the weight of winter's hold.
In frozen fields, we find the flowers,
Shining spirits, brave and bold.

Luminescent Dreams Under a Quiet Moon

Beneath the sky, a silver sheen,
Dreams awaken in cool night air.
The world transforms, serene,
In the moonlight’s gentle care.

Pale reflections on the snow,
Guided by the stars above.
In winter’s calm, we start to grow,
Finding warmth in every love.

As shadows blend with quiet light,
The heart beats slow, a tender song.
In this space of peaceful night,
We belong, we can’t be wrong.

Whispered secrets in the breeze,
Echo softly in the dark.
With each breath, the spirit frees,
In dreams where winter leaves its mark.

Luminance of a Winter's sigh

Beneath the pale and frosty sky,
The whispers dance on chilled night air.
Each breath a cloud, a soft goodbye,
As stars shimmer in their sweet despair.

The moon, a lantern, softly glows,
Illuminating snow-draped pines.
In stillness, nature's beauty flows,
A silent hymn where dream divines.

A world adorned in crystal lace,
With laughter bright, and hearts set free.
Each flake a memory in this space,
Of warmth held close, a reverie.

The winter wind, a gentle song,
Carries tales of love and light.
In frosted air, we all belong,
Together twinkling through the night.

Through every sigh, a promise made,
In whispers soft, the season's breath.
While in the quiet, colors fade,
We find our joy, in life, in death.

Dreams Entwined in Frozen Light

In twilight's arms, the dreams take flight,
Entwined beneath the stars so bright.
Each shadow plays, a fleeting sight,
In frozen realms where hearts unite.

A tapestry of snowflakes spun,
Whispers of night, where sorrows run.
With every step, the silence won,
In moonlit paths, our souls are fun.

The winter's breath, a gentle tease,
In every sigh, a frosty breeze.
As dreams cascade like autumn leaves,
We chase the night, our hearts at ease.

Stars twinkle like a distant fire,
Each glimmered hope takes us higher.
In frozen light, we dare aspire,
To find the warmth, our one desire.

In this embrace, where time is still,
The world transformed, we weave our thrill.
With frozen dreams our hearts fulfill,
While softening the winter's chill.

Portrait of Chill and Glow

A portrait crafted by winter's hand,
With hues of blue, and whispers grand.
The chill of night, a velvet strand,
Enfolding all in magic's brand.

The glow of fire, a warmth profound,
Each flickering flame holds dreams unbound.
In velvet airs, where peace is found,
Our laughter flows, a joyful sound.

Beneath the moon, the shadows play,
As snowflakes swirl in a soft ballet.
Within this frame, we drift away,
Where chill meets glow, our hearts will stay.

A canvas rich with frosty gleam,
Entwined in twilight's gentle dream.
In chilly breath, we share a theme,
Of love and light, a radiant beam.

As morning breaks, the sun will rise,
To melt the frost, unveil the skies.
In every glow, the chill belies,
A portrait rich with sweet goodbyes.

Eventide in a Winter's Embrace

As eventide paints the world in grey,
We gather close, our fears at bay.
In winter's arms, we find our way,
With every breath, come what may.

The twilight hush, a soft caress,
Wraps us in peace, a warm finesse.
Within the stillness, we find our rest,
In love's embrace, we feel the best.

Under the gaze of the fading light,
We share our dreams through the quiet night.
In every heartbeat, a frozen flight,
Together we chase away the fright.

With stars above so vast and bright,
We ponder life, what's wrong, what's right.
In winter's cold, we hold on tight,
Creating warmth, igniting light.

A tapestry of memories spun,
In winter's embrace, we are as one.
Each moment cherished, never done,
Together, forever, we have won.

Glistening Veils of White

Blankets of snow fall so bright,
Covering earth in pure delight.
Glistening veils, a soft embrace,
Nature dons her quiet grace.

Whispers of winter in the air,
Each flake dances without a care.
Silent nights with stars aglow,
Under moonlight, dreams will flow.

Footprints trail where none have been,
In this world, so calm, serene.
Gentle winds through branches glide,
Joyful secrets they confide.

Crystal crystals, a jeweled ground,
In the stillness, peace is found.
Frozen moments, oh, so rare,
Magic lingers everywhere.

As daylight fades, shadows creep,
In this season, spirits leap.
Glistening veils of winter's cheer,
A splendid sight, so crystal clear.

Tender Caress of Winter's Breath

A gentle sigh from winter's mouth,
Drifts softly in from the cold south.
Breath of ice, a fleeting kiss,
In its chill, there's quiet bliss.

Trees adorned with frosty lace,
Nature's art, a timeless grace.
Every branch a story tells,
In the hush where silence dwells.

Snowflakes whirl like whispered dreams,
In the glow of midday beams.
Tender caress, a soft embrace,
Winter’s breath leaves a trace.

As twilight glimmers in the skies,
Stars awaken, brightly rise.
In this world, time stands still,
Hearts are warmed, a joy to fill.

Moments captured, crisp and clear,
Winter's tender, sweet veneer.
With each breath, a fleeting song,
In this wonder, we belong.

Where the Stars Meet the Snow

Up above, the stars do gleam,
Twinkling bright like a waking dream.
Below, the snow lies fresh and deep,
In this silence, nature sleeps.

Footfalls soft on the powdery white,
Under the gaze of the glowing night.
Where the stars meet the snow so fine,
Magic weaves through each line.

Winds whisper secrets, soft and low,
In the moonlight, shadows grow.
Dreams take flight like a snowflake's fall,
In this land, we find it all.

Magic moments, the world so still,
Hearts embrace the winter chill.
In the calm, a world reborn,
As night fades into the morn.

Together, the earth and sky align,
Where the stars meet the snow divine.
In this winter's tender hold,
Beauty lies in stories told.

Moonlit Caress on Cold Ground

Moonlit whispers on cold ground,
As the stillness wraps around.
Silver gleams upon the night,
Enveloping the world in light.

Frosty sparkles in the air,
Nature's magic everywhere.
Underneath the starry shroud,
Dreams awaken, echo loud.

Crisp and clean, the evening glows,
In this peace, a refuge grows.
Moonlit caress, a soft descent,
Filling hearts with sweet content.

Each shadow dances, plays its part,
Winter’s chill warms the heart.
In the silence, we find peace,
As frigid nights provide release.

Gazing upwards at the glow,
Underneath the world so slow.
Moonlit beauty, a wondrous sight,
Guides us gently into night.

Flickering Dreams in the Frosty Night

In the stillness, whispers flow,
Flickers dance, a soft aglow.
Stars above in silence gleam,
Chasing softly fleeting dream.

Beneath the blanket, shadows play,
Winter's chill, a gentle sway.
Each breath a cloud, a secret shared,
In the night, none are scared.

Echoes of laughter, soft and free,
In this realm, just you and me.
Frosty flakes fall like sighs,
Painting stories in the skies.

Branches creak with ancient tales,
As the moonlight softly pales.
The beauty of the frozen scene,
Awakens all that's left unseen.

With every flicker, hope ignites,
In this calm, all wrongs feel right.
Flickering dreams under the night,
Lead us forth to morning light.

Woven Hearts on Icebound Paths

On the ice where whispers blend,
Two souls meet, hearts transcend.
Frozen rivers hold their spark,
Together lighting up the dark.

Every glance, a story told,
Hands entwined, warmth from the cold.
Through the night, our laughter flows,
In the stillness, love grows.

Footsteps trace a tender line,
Etched in snow, pure and divine.
With every turn, joy unfolds,
Woven hearts, a bond that holds.

Beneath the moon's soft embrace,
Nature sings, a sacred space.
In this chill, our spirits dance,
Together in a frozen trance.

Icebound paths, no fear, no rush,
In the quiet, we feel the hush.
Woven hearts, forever shared,
In this world, love is declared.

Touched by Winter's Glistening Breath

In the dawn of frosty morn,
Eager whispers greet the dawn.
Glistening breath, a silken touch,
Nature’s magic, felt so much.

Every flake a kiss, divine,
Painting landscapes, pure, benign.
Breath of winter, soft and light,
Wraps the world in quiet white.

Branches bow with crystal weight,
Nature pauses, holds its fate.
In this stillness, we are found,
Touched by beauty all around.

Each moment's fleeting, yet so bright,
Captured in the morning light.
A gentle hush, so warm, so deep,
In winter's hold, our hearts do leap.

Touched by love in frosty air,
In this ballet, none compare.
Through glistening nights, we'll tread,
In winter's breath, our dreams are spread.

Enigmatic Conversations Under Moonlit Frost

Underneath the silver glow,
Conversations dance, soft and slow.
Moonlit frost, a perfect guise,
Secrets shared under starry skies.

Whispers float on chilly breeze,
In this moment, time can freeze.
Veils of night, so mysterious,
With each word, the world is curious.

Eyes that sparkle, minds that dream,
Caught in this ethereal scheme.
Frosty silence, soft as snow,
In this unity, hearts will grow.

Together lost in paper moons,
Dancing to our silent tunes.
Every shadow speaks of grace,
Enigmas found in this embrace.

Underneath the stars so bright,
Conversations dance through the night.
With the frost, our spirits soar,
In this realm, we seek for more.

Hushed Shadows of the Frost

In the still of night, whispers glide,
Softly wrapped in winter's pride.
Silent echoes through the trees,
Carried gently on the breeze.

Moonlight dances on the ground,
Painting shadows all around.
Every flake a silent prayer,
Cloaked in magic, cold and rare.

Footsteps muffled, hearts in tune,
Guided by the silver moon.
Nature's breath, a warming sigh,
In the hush of frost, we lie.

Frozen whispers, secrets kept,
In the realm where dreams are swept.
Hold the stillness, let it grow,
In the shadow's quiet glow.

Eternal night will softly fade,
As dawn breaks with tender jade.
Yet in frosty silence found,
Hushed shadows roam, still unbound.

Elysium Under the Icebound Sky

Beneath a dome of icy dreams,
Where sunlight glimmers, softly beams.
A quiet world, white and pure,
In stillness, we feel secure.

Crystal rivers flow with grace,
Reflecting nature's gentle face.
Winds of winter weave a song,
That calls to hearts where they belong.

Frozen landscapes, vast and wide,
In this haven, joys reside.
Through sparkling woods, the silence sings,
Of peace that pure elysium brings.

Stars like diamonds, bright and high,
Light the way through night's soft sigh.
Every breath, a fleeting bliss,
In the world's cold, warmest kiss.

Underneath the sky so clear,
All our worries disappear.
In this realm of ice and light,
Hope and dreams take wing in flight.

The Enchantment of Frozen Light

Glistening crystals, fairy dust,
Enchantment dances, life is just.
Every sparkle, magic's bond,
In this winter's wonderland.

Branches heavy, bending low,
Cradling secrets, soft and slow.
Shadows flicker, bright and bold,
In this tale that time has told.

Reflections whisper, tell a tale,
Of starlit dreams where hopes prevail.
Nature dons her sparkling dress,
In frozen light, we feel blessed.

Moments captured, breath held tight,
Lost in the glow of crystal light.
Here in the still, a heart can heal,
In the magic, we can feel.

When the dawn breaks, all will change,
Yet in this moment, nothing’s strange.
For time stands still, a gentle fight,
In the enchantment of frozen light.

Crystal Tears on Snowy Limbs

Upon the bough, soft tears descend,
Droplets glisten, nature's blend.
Frosty sighs in twilight's grace,
Layered pearls on winter's face.

Snowy limbs, a tender embrace,
Hold the crystal tears in place.
Each a story, softly spun,
Underneath the pale, cold sun.

Time slows down, the world still weeps,
In the silence, beauty sleeps.
Nature's heart, a fragile show,
Where the gentle glimmers flow.

Every drop, a fleeting dream,
Caught in light's soft, silver beam.
A fleeting kiss from sky to ground,
In this wonder, peace is found.

With the night, the tears will freeze,
Transforming hearts with quiet ease.
In the morning's softest gleam,
Whispers of a crystal dream.

A Tapestry of Winter Whispers

In the hushed embrace of snowy nights,
Frosted branches hold soft lights.
Whispers weave through the icy air,
Stories of warmth, beyond compare.

Moonlight dances on the frozen ground,
Echoes of silence, a peace profound.
Blankets of white cover the earth,
A sacred pause for winter's mirth.

Footprints trace a delicate path,
Children laughing, enjoying the wrath.
Nature's lullaby, softly it sings,
Hope and joy that winter brings.

Stars twinkle like diamonds in the night,
Casting shadows that shimmer bright.
Among the trees, the stillness grows,
In winter's embrace, serenity flows.

Beneath the frost, life waits in dreams,
A tapestry stitched with delicate seams.
As time drifts slowly on snowy flights,
Winter whispers of magical nights.

Radiance Beneath the Icy Veil

Under the frost, a glow persists,
Whispers of warmth in the cold mists.
Glistening flakes in the pale moonlight,
Nature's canvas, exquisite and bright.

Trees wear coats of glittering charms,
Beneath the chill, the world disarms.
Hidden colors in the ice reside,
Fragrant dreams where spirits glide.

A flicker of life beneath the snow,
Soft and gentle, a warm inner glow.
Encapsulated beauty, silent and true,
Winter's breath, a miracle anew.

Silently falling, the snowflakes twirl,
In the stillness, emotions unfurl.
A soft radiance in shadows cast,
Hope for tomorrow, in moments past.

Beneath the icy veil, dreams awaken,
A radiant warmth, never forsaken.
In each crystal, a story spun,
Whispers of life beneath the sun.

Chilling Beauty in Soft Radiance

Shimmering frost on a quiet morn,
Nature's grace in silence born.
Each flake a thought, a moment to keep,
In chilling beauty, the world lies deep.

Icicles hang like jeweled art,
A tranquil spell that steals the heart.
Softly the winds through branches play,
They murmur secrets of winter's sway.

Underneath the glow of the pale sun,
A realm of soft whispers has begun.
In every shadow and sparkling light,
Beauty unfolds, a magical sight.

Embers of warmth in the crisp, cool air,
Every breath speaks of wonder rare.
Moments captured in delicate frost,
In winter's art, we’re never lost.

Around the fire, stories unfold,
Of chilling beauty, brave and bold.
In the depths of winter, we find release,
A soft radiance, a heart's sweet peace.

Quiet Repose in Glimmering White

A blanket of white on the sleeping ground,
In quiet repose, the world is found.
Soft breaths of winter embrace the trees,
Rustling leaves whisper in the freeze.

Shadows stretch long in the fading light,
Glimmering edges that dance and ignite.
Peaceful moments, serene and bright,
In the heart of winter, everything feels right.

A symphony plays in the chilly air,
Nature's music, soothing and rare.
Each breath a cloud, drifting and free,
In a world of stillness, just you and me.

Frosty patterns on windowpanes,
Echoes of laughter in soft refrains.
Memory lingers in the frosted night,
Life waits patiently for spring's first light.

Stars whisper secrets in the deep blue skies,
With every twinkle, a dream softly flies.
In quiet repose, we find our way,
In winter's embrace, here we will stay.

Fragments of Light in Frozen Infinity

In the stillness of the night,
Flickers dance like dreams in flight.
Whispers of ice, soft and bright,
Fragments of light in frozen sight.

A crystalline world, pure and clear,
Each glimmer holds a secret near.
Shadows shift, a hint of cheer,
Frozen wonders we hold dear.

Silent echoes of days gone by,
Reflections shimmer, catch the eye.
Time suspended, like a sigh,
Beneath the vast, unending sky.

Within this realm of frost and gleam,
Nature crafts a gentle dream.
A cosmic dance, a flowing stream,
In frozen silence, we redeem.

So let us wander, hand in hand,
Through a world so bright, so grand.
In the frosty air we stand,
Fragments of light upon the sand.

A Tapestry of Ice and Light

Woven threads of silver ice,
Patterns glinting, oh so nice.
Underneath the starry skies,
A tapestry that never lies.

Crystals form a delicate lace,
Nature's touch, a fleeting grace.
In the chill, we find our place,
Embraced in winter's tender space.

With every dawn, new layers shine,
A silent witness, pure divine.
Upon the earth, a soft design,
A dance of light, a love so fine.

Paths of frost beneath our feet,
Echoes of a world so sweet.
In this beauty, hearts will meet,
A harmony that's pure and neat.

So let the cold and warmth entwine,
In nature's art, so rare, so fine.
Together we'll explore, align,
In this tapestry, your hand in mine.

Luminous Traces of Frosty Whimsy

Glistening trails through snow-lit night,
Whimsy dances, pure delight.
Each breath a cloud, a frosty bite,
Luminous traces, soft and light.

Underneath the moon's soft glow,
Dreams awaken, spirits flow.
In the air, a gentle show,
Magic whispers, telling all we know.

Wonders spark in silence deep,
Secrets that the shadows keep.
As the night bids us to leap,
Into dreams where we can sleep.

Frosted branches, twinkling bright,
Nature's laughter, pure and right.
In this realm of joy and fright,
We share our warmth against the night.

So let’s embrace this tender phase,
Find the joy in winter's haze.
In the frosty air, we blaze,
With luminous traces through our days.

Stars Whispering Through the Winter Haze

In the hush of winter's breath,
Stars are talking, life and death.
Through the haze, they weave a thread,
A tale of dreams, of light widespread.

Softly shining, secrets shared,
Every twinkle, every glare.
In this moment, souls are bared,
Underneath the sky, we dare.

Frosty winds like whispers call,
Magic found in nature’s thrall.
In the dark, we rise and fall,
As the stars around us sprawl.

Each constellation tells a tale,
Of distant worlds beyond the pale.
In their glow, we will not fail,
To find our way, to set our sail.

So let us wander, night so bright,
Feel the warmth in winter's bite.
As we dance in starlit light,
In the haze, we’ll find our right.

Frosty Breath of the Twilight

The twilight whispers in the chill,
Breath of frost upon the hill.
Stars awaken, soft and bright,
In the dance of fading light.

A silver mist begins to weave,
Through the branches, as they grieve.
Nature holds her breath so still,
In the grasp of winter's will.

Moonlight glistens on the snow,
Footprints linger, soft and slow.
In this calm, the world feels right,
Frosty breath of coming night.

Beneath the sky, a quiet song,
Nature's lullaby, soft and long.
Winds of change, they softly call,
And swallow shadows, one and all.

In the chill, a warm embrace,
Winter’s arms, a gentle space.
Time stands still, as dreams take flight,
In the frosty breath of twilight.

Serenity in the Shimmering Silence

In the woods where echoes cease,
Shimmering frost brings tranquil peace.
Every flake, a whisper clear,
Drapes the world in silver sheer.

Gentle glows of moonlit rays,
Paint the night in softest ways.
Silence sings, a hymn divine,
Dancing shadows intertwine.

Stars above, like jewels bright,
Gaze upon this soft delight.
In the stillness, dreams arrive,
In serenity, we feel alive.

Every breath, a frosty sigh,
Moments linger, drift and fly.
Embrace the cold, let it mend,
As we find a way to blend.

In the heart of winter’s breath,
Lies a peace beyond all death.
Nature's echo, pure dispel,
In the shimmering silence, we dwell.

A Symphony of Icy Serenades

Underneath a blanket white,
Nature sings with pure delight.
Icy notes in breezes wend,
A symphony that won't suspend.

Frozen lakes like mirrors gleam,
Reflecting every twilight dream.
In the hush, the world transforms,
Into rhythms, soft and warm.

Branches sway in frosty airs,
Tales of winter, love declares.
Each note drips like crystal rain,
A melody that soothes the pain.

Stars take part in this grand play,
Guiding hearts along the way.
Every whisper, every sound,
Of ice and snow is beauty found.

In the glimmer, warmth ignites,
A symphony of winter nights.
Listen close, let silence guide,
Through the icy serenades, we glide.

Caresses of Glimmering Frost

Morning breaks with glimmering light,
Frosted whispers, pure and bright.
A gentle touch upon the ground,
In the hush, a beauty found.

Each blade of grass, a jeweled dress,
Nature’s art in soft excess.
Glimmers dance upon the trees,
Carried softly by the breeze.

Underneath the winter sun,
Every chill leads to the fun.
As the world begins to glow,
Frosted caresses, soft and slow.

In this moment, hearts align,
Touch of frost, a love divine.
With every shimmer, joy is tossed,
In the caresses of glimmering frost.

Winter's breath, a tender art,
Holds the secrets of the heart.
In these glistening hours lost,
We find solace in the frost.

Glimmering Moments in the Chilling Air

In the quiet of the dawn,
Snowflakes dance, a gentle call.
Whispers of the winter wind,
Moments bright, yet fleeting all.

Frosted branches, shimmering white,
A world wrapped in crystal grace.
Breath like mist, a fleeting sight,
Time stands still in this embrace.

Glistening roofs, soft and bright,
Children laugh, their voices soar.
Chasing dreams in pure delight,
Hands held high, they ask for more.

Underneath the pale gray sky,
Nature's canvas, cold and bare.
Yet within, the sparks fly high,
In glimmering moments we share.

Evening falls, the stars ignite,
A blanket soft, the earth does wear.
Deep in silence, heart takes flight,
In the chill, love finds its lair.

Embracing the Frosted Serengeti

Underneath the icy stars,
The plains stretch wide, so still, so bright.
Creatures roam, like ancient scars,
In the frosted, pale moonlight.

Grasslands wrapped in silver dreams,
Whispers echo between the trees.
Nature's heart, it softly gleams,
With every step, a gentle freeze.

Footprints trace the glistening ground,
As shadows dance in frosty air.
Life awakens all around,
In this stillness, warmth we share.

Roaming herds, a sight to see,
Majestic figures bound in grace.
In this white, they roam so free,
In the chill, they find their place.

Each moment carved, a work of art,
Frosted whispers fill the space.
This frozen land, a beating heart,
In chilly nights, we find embrace.

Dappled Light on the Winter's Palette

Morning breaks with golden rays,
Dancing through the branches bare.
A canvas fresh, the world displays,
Winter's palette, beyond compare.

The sunlight glints on frozen streams,
Sparkling like a million stars.
Nature weaves its silent dreams,
Painting whispers in the bars.

Shadows play on the sparkling snow,
Footfalls soft, the world feels new.
With every step, the grasses bow,
Underneath the sky so blue.

Trees stand tall, adorned in frost,
Their elegance, a sight so rare.
In this beauty, we find what's lost,
In dappled light, we find our care.

As daylight fades and shadows blend,
The colors shift, a soft caress.
In winter's heart, we start to mend,
With hues of love, we feel the bless.

The Soft Glow of Icy Caresses

In the stillness of the night,
Moonlight bathes the world in blue.
Every flake, a jewel of light,
Whispers linger, cold and true.

Frosted windows, patterns weave,
Nature's art, a tender sigh.
Each breath catches, hearts believe,
In the cold, we learn to fly.

Branches laden, heavy sighs,
The world wrapped in a silver quilt.
Soft glow dances in our eyes,
In these nights, our dreams are built.

Shadows stretch beneath the trees,
With every step, a soft embrace.
The air carries winter’s breeze,
In icy caresses, find your place.

Eager hearts beneath the stars,
Warmth ignites as snowflakes fall.
In this beauty, near and far,
The soft glow unites us all.

Whispering Pines Under the Ice

Beneath the trees where shadows play,
A hushed breath lingers, night holds sway.
The whispers call on frosty air,
As time slows down, beyond compare.

Glittering shards in moonlit glow,
Dance like spirits, soft and slow.
Pines wear coats of shimmering lace,
In winter's clasp, a still embrace.

A distant echo of the night,
The world transformed in soft twilight.
Nature holds her secrets tight,
In tranquil realms, pure and bright.

Snowflakes kiss the frozen ground,
In every hush, magic is found.
The air is crisp, the silence deep,
A lullaby that lulls to sleep.

Walking paths where dreams unfold,
Stories whispered, secrets told.
Through whispering pines, we find our way,
Under the ice, where shadows play.

Crystal Arcadia and Heartfelt Embrace

In a land where crystals gleam,
The heart awakes, a quiet dream.
Snowflakes twirl with grace divine,
In icy splendor, love will shine.

Every glimmer, a sparkling note,
In winter's song, our spirits float.
Warmth ignites the coldest night,
In this arcadia, hearts take flight.

Embraced by frost, we roam the scene,
Each breath a cloud, pure and serene.
Hands entwined, we weave a tale,
Through icy gusts, we will not pale.

The stars above, like diamonds bright,
Guide us gently through the night.
In every shimmer, a promise lies,
In crystal dreams, love never dies.

So let us wander, hearts ablaze,
In crystal arcadia, lost in a daze.
Through every flake, our bond we trace,
In winter’s warmth, a heartfelt embrace.

Velvet Touch of a Winter's Night

The velvet night drapes soft and low,
Whispers of winds, gentle and slow.
Stars twinkle like frost-kissed dreams,
In a world kissed by silver beams.

Cloaked in shadows, we find our way,
Through snowy paths, where spirits play.
In quiet corners, the moonlight gleams,
Illuminating the heart's soft themes.

The chill embraces, yet warms the soul,
A tender touch that makes us whole.
In winter's breath, time stands still,
A tranquil peace, a void to fill.

Glimmers of hope weave through the night,
As dreams awaken in soft light.
Each heartbeat echoes through the trees,
In the velvet dark, our spirits seize.

Together we dance on the frosted ground,
In the silence, our hearts resound.
In the velvet touch of winter's grace,
We find our haven, a sacred space.

Frosty Caress of the Quiet Dawn

The dawn awakes with gentle grace,
A frosty caress, a soft embrace.
Shadows linger, but light draws near,
In morning's glow, the world is clear.

Each blade of grass adorned with frost,
A fleeting beauty, never lost.
Birds begin their whispered song,
In the quiet, where we belong.

With every breath, the chill ignites,
The dawn reveals our dreams in flights.
In hues of pink and pale blue skies,
A canvas painted with love's goodbyes.

The world awakens, soft and bright,
In frosty moments, take delight.
Unity found in nature's call,
In the quiet dawn, we embrace it all.

As the sun climbs, shadows fade,
Marking places where hope is laid.
In the frosty touch, a new day’s dawn,
A gentle start, the past withdrawn.

Dreaming in the Dusk’s Glow

In the twilight's soft embrace,
Shadows dance with gentle grace.
Whispers of the night unfold,
Stories in the dusk retold.

Stars begin their nightly show,
Casting dreams in hues that glow.
The air holds a sweet delight,
As day surrenders to the night.

Crickets sing a soothing song,
While the world fades, all feels wrong.
In my heart, the warmth remains,
Alive within the evening's chains.

Moonlight spills like molten gold,
Painting dreams as tales grow old.
Each twinkle brings a silent sigh,
Lingering where dreams may lie.

Seeking solace in the dark,
Where the night ignites a spark.
In the quiet, visions soar,
Waiting now, forevermore.

Celestial Glimmers on Snowy Plains

Beneath a blanket pure and white,
Stars reflect the crisp moonlight.
Whispers travel on the breeze,
As shadows dance among the trees.

The world is hushed, a calm embrace,
Celestial glimmers find their place.
Each flake a wish, each breath a dream,
Sparkling softly, like a stream.

Footprints mark the endless night,
Leading where the heart takes flight.
In the stillness, joy will rise,
Underneath the starry skies.

The frosty air, a gentle kiss,
Wrapping hopes in winter's bliss.
In this realm where silence reigns,
A tapestry of icy chains.

Glimmers paint the world in gold,
Tales of warmth in the cold.
In the snowy plains, we find,
Heaven's gift to humankind.

A Reverie in Silvery White

In silvery shadows softly lain,
Dreams emerge from winter's strain.
Softly glows the moonlit night,
Casting warmth in pure delight.

A reverie drifts through the air,
Fleeting thoughts, moments rare.
Whispered secrets, soft and clear,
Echo in the silence near.

Frosty petals softly fall,
Wrapping beauty in a thrall.
Nature's whispers beckon low,
In the stillness, hearts will grow.

Past the shadows, dreams descend,
Guided by the night's sweet blend.
Floating softly through the night,
In the moon's warm, tender light.

Each twirl of snow, a gentle flight,
Turns the dark to purest white.
In this dream, we find our place,
Wrapped in winter's soft embrace.

Frosted Petals in Moon’s Glow

Frosted petals softly gleam,
Caught within a silver dream.
Underneath the moon’s soft gaze,
Nature’s beauty, hearts ablaze.

Each bloom whispers tales untold,
In the night where dreams unfold.
Moonlight bathes them, pure and bright,
Crafting magic in the night.

The chill enhances every hue,
As the world transforms anew.
Silent moments, deep and wide,
In this realm we gracefully glide.

Glistening leaves join the dance,
Wrapped in winter’s sweet romance.
Frosted petals, calm and slow,
In the beauty of moon’s glow.

A tapestry of light and ice,
Bringing dreams that feel so nice.
In this night, the heart will flow,
Through the frost and moonlight's glow.

A Blank Canvas of White Peace

The snowflakes dance like dreams,
A hush falls on the ground,
Each step a gentle whisper,
Wrapped in a world unbound.

A canvas pure and endless,
Where hopes can gently bloom,
In silence, hearts find solace,
Beneath the winter's loom.

The trees wear coats of crystal,
With branches soft and bright,
Nature's art unfolding,
In morning's tender light.

Peace blankets all around us,
In every flake, a prayer,
For moments filled with wonder,
As winter's breath we share.

A blank canvas of white peace,
Invites a deeper sigh,
In the tranquility of snow,
Underneath the vast blue sky.

The Light Beneath the Frosted Veil

A shimmer hides in shadows,
Beneath the frosted glass,
Giving life to frozen branches,
While time begins to pass.

The world wrapped in its whiteness,
Holds secrets still untold,
Yet warmth resides beneath it,
In stories woven bold.

Each crystal glimmers softly,
In twilight's gentle glow,
A promise of the springtime,
Waiting 'neath the snow.

The light breaks through the silence,
A dance of hope in frost,
For every chilly moment,
New dreams cannot be lost.

The light beneath the frosted veil,
Awakens spirit bright,
In winter's heartfelt grasp,
We find our way to light.

Celestial Shards and Heartfelt Shadows

Upon the night sky's canvas,
Stars scatter like confetti,
Celestial shards of wonder,
In dreams, we find our levy.

Heartfelt shadows dance around,
In whispers soft and low,
Tales told by the moonlight,
As winter winds do blow.

Each twinkle holds a secret,
A wish upon a breeze,
In cosmos' vast expanse,
Our hearts begin to freeze.

Yet even in the darkness,
We find a spark of grace,
In every shining treasure,
A warm and glowing face.

Celestial shards and heartfelt shadows,
Together they ignite,
In the quiet of the evening,
Our hopes take graceful flight.

Whimsy in the Midst of Cold

In snowball fights with laughter,
Joy bursts like fireworks bright,
As children play and wander,
Through winter's playful night.

A snowman stands in glory,
With buttons made of coal,
He guards the dreams of many,
In this chill that feels so whole.

Flakes swirl like little dancers,
Each twirl a fleeting thrill,
In wonder's pure embrace,
We chase the snow downhill.

The winter air is crisp and clear,
With magic in each breath,
A world where whimsy lingers,
Enveloping in depth.

Whimsy in the midst of cold,
Reminds us to be bold,
To find delight in moments,
As glowing as the gold.

Silvery Hush on Snow-blanketed Ground

A silvery hush lies over the land,
Cocooned in winter's soft, gentle hand.
Footsteps muffled, a world reposed,
Under the blanket where stillness flows.

Pine trees draped in a shimmering white,
Stars twinkle softly in the still of night.
Moonlight dances on crystals bright,
Nature's canvas, pure and white.

Hushed whispers drift on the frosty air,
The earth takes a breath, a moment rare.
In this silence, dreams are found,
In the silvery hush on snow-blanketed ground.

Time seems to pause, within the chill,
The heart beats softly, in quiet thrill.
Each flake a story, each drift a sound,
Embraced in peace, all worries unbound.

Beneath the vast, starry dome above,
A world asleep, cradled in love.
Wrapped in a beauty that knows no end,
In silvered stillness, the heart may mend.

Midnight's Whispers Entwined in Frost

At midnight's hour, the frost takes hold,
Whispers of secrets, soft and bold.
Tales of warmth in a cold embrace,
Moonlit magic adorns the space.

Each breath a cloud, in the cool of night,
Stars above, twinkling, a wondrous sight.
Frozen branches, nature’s art,
In the stillness, warmth fills the heart.

A silver veil over fields does lay,
Guiding the dreams that drift away.
The nightingale sings a lullaby sweet,
In frost-kissed silence, where shadows meet.

The world holds its breath in this winter's glow,
In every corner, soft whispers flow.
Wrapped in the magic of night’s embrace,
In frost and whispers, we find our place.

As dawn approaches, colors ignite,
But for now, let's linger in the night.
With hearts entwined in frosty delight,
We cherish the magic till morning light.

Whispers of Winter's Glow

Gentle whispers float on the breeze,
Winter’s embrace, a chill that frees.
Softly glowing through frosted trees,
Hearts are warmed with simple ease.

Each flake that falls, a delicate dance,
Nature’s beauty given a chance.
With every shimmer, a soft romance,
In winter’s arms, lost in a trance.

The world wears a coat of brilliant white,
Under the watch of the silvered night.
With every breath, a tale unfolds,
Of whispered secrets that winter holds.

As shadows twirl by the moon's soft light,
The wild embraces the stillness of night.
There's magic woven through trees aglow,
In the quietude, winter’s whispers flow.

With every dawn, the stories will grow,
Of shimmering landscapes, pure as snow.
A tender reminder of nature’s grace,
In the whispers of winter’s embrace.

Glistening Veils of Frost

Glistening veils drape the earth below,
Each crystal sparkles, a radiant show.
Whispers of winter soft on the tongue,
Echoes of beauty, forever young.

Underneath stars, the world stands still,
Nature reclines on a snow-covered hill.
Frosted dreams in the cool night air,
Awakening wonder everywhere.

Branches adorned in a lacy frost,
The beauty of winter, never lost.
In the hush of night, time seems to flow,
In the glistening veils of frost, we grow.

Each flake is a promise, a story to tell,
Of love and warmth where coldness fell.
Boundless as stars that shimmer above,
We revel in nature, we're wrapped in love.

As dawn approaches, the colors ignite,
Yet still, we cherish the magic of night.
For in every frost-laden breath we breathe,
Lies the glistening wonder that weaves and weaves.

www.ingramcontent.com/pod-product-compliance
Ingram Content Group UK Ltd.
Pitfield, Milton Keynes, MK11 3LW, UK
UKHW031941151224
452382UK00006B/199

9 789916 793602